T0209622

SONG OF
Sarahrose

SARAHROSE

authorHOUSE®

AuthorHouse™
1663 Liberty Drive
Bloomington, IN 47403
www.authorhouse.com
Phone: 1 (800) 839-8640

Published by AuthorHouse 11/14/2019

ISBN: 978-1-7283-3455-4 (sc)
ISBN: 978-1-7283-3454-7 (e)

Print information available on the last page.

This book is printed on acid-free paper.

Dedication

This book is dedicated to every person in my life that supports my growth, and appreciates the expressions of my heart. Thank you for showing your love, and fueling me to continue spreading my message!

My prayer

May I see myself

The way that you see me

May I love myself

The way that you love me

May I live in the light

That you shine on me

May I touch someone else

The way you have touched me

Eyes

Can you see my pain

It's hidden in my eyes

In my world there's rain

Covering over my cries

Build I must a future

Forget I must the past

As I search for understanding

I better make it fast

Can you see my pain

It's here showing in my eyes

I should not be ashamed

Everybody cries

Happy birthday to me

Happy birthday to me...

This harsh cruel world,

Just threw me in.

So full of innocence,

So full of life.

There was hope in those big bright eyes,

There was a beauty in her soul.

Even through the worst of times

She smiled her way through the pain.

Dreamed away while stuck in a world that rejected her.

A family that chose to take her,

Then failed to give her the love she deserved...

The love every child longs for,

The security every child needs.

Is this world as bad as it seemed?

A home filled with filth, and clutter, and abuse.

Even school just proved that everyone is cruel!

Still her soul stayed beautiful,

Her heart eager to love.

Always forgiving since nobody is perfect,

This world as an adult isn't any nicer!

It's staining the soul of that big blue eyed girl

Her smile isn't as big, her heart isn't as open

All faith in humanity has disappeared

This world is leaving her empty and broken...

Happy birthday to me, with that little girl still in there

Wishing somebody cared...

The spice of life

The spice of life that has kept me strong,

That had me going for so long,

Has let me down.

As time goes by and my soul cries,

I tell myself lies.

I have felt my demise.

I have felt my demise.

Every time I close my eyes,

It's like a piece of me cries for belonging,

Or just a hint of care.

Though every time I turn around there is nothing there,

But despair.

I know better than I walk and you can hear it when I talk.

As I follow the wrong leader

And he leads me deeper into my destruction.

The battle within my mind only gets worse with passing time,

As I get more lost in my worry...

It's nothing new for this lost soul.

Struggling always is getting old as my heart is growing cold.

From all this corruption,

Our own fatal destruction.

Always working on my construction.

Getting stuck in the web I have woven.

My happiness so long ago was stolen,

Always I must keep trying to remain strong.

We only live so long.

It's never too late to find our fate,

Though it's hard to start to change...

It's hard to walk away from that lie of comfort and stability.

To leave would be uncertain and scary,

But he is not part of my destiny.

That is not what God has planned for me.

The spice of life that I embraced,

That gave life meaning,

Put a glow on my face.

That glow has disappeared,

I still have faith.

I will never say it's too late.

My inner self has been hidden away.

I forgot who I am,

Started losing myself more every day,

And in every way.

I gotta get away and find my spice, my soul.

One day maybe I will feel whole.

Maze

I'm destroying my temple

The temple God had built

Every gasp of air I take

I'm consumed and fueled with guilt

The maze of my life is too big

The labyrinth is broad and tall

Every new path I choose to take

I'm unsure was the right one at all

I stand to fall, but I stand tall

If only I could see above the wall

To see the maze and find my way

Because I feel that I'm in the wrong place

Please my Lord, guide my way

Here is nowhere

Determination and frustration.

Corruption and destruction.

As I destroy my temple,

As I corrupt my life.

Some say that life is simple,

Then why is it a constant fight?

Where nothing ever seems right.

A struggle to quiet my mind and sleep at night.

I am my own harshest critic,

Shaming and ridiculing myself.

It's like I'm never finished,

Like I will never feel well.

I can never be my full potential,

Never be my best.

I'm too stained by this world.

It's not easy being a broken girl.

With all the commotion our emotions take over.

We're forced to feel what men ignore,

Looked down on and used as men's whores.

All these frustrations I cannot ignore.

Tears puddle this path I take.

I cannot mistake this pain,

I cannot ignore this hurt.

As I shuffle forwards slowly,

Kicking up the dirt....

Of the road to nowhere,

Here is nowhere

Lessons

My life is set up with obstacles.

Some hurdles, some struggles,

Some fun, some failures.

In the end it makes me grow stronger.

Each lesson is what it is,

And I get what I get.

No matter how much it hurts.

I can't let pain win.

There is always the good and opportunity in our faces.

We can always love to live.

It just takes a good attitude,

Love and patience.

We all get tired of waiting.

I should start taking steps closer every day.

Earn a good mind,

Reflected from a strong soul,

All fueled from a kind heart.

I will not let myself fall apart.

I've worked so hard in this challenged life,

At this point I will keep doing right.

I didn't realize I was blind until suddenly,

I had sight.

Knowing now, I will be alright.

I'm not just crossing my fingers and saying a prayer.

I'm doing what I've got to do,

Loving my life the best that I can.

Learning my lessons,

Being there any way that I can.

Knowing when we think we can't,

We can.

Out of place

We've awakened the beast and now he must feed.

No matter how hard you try you still feel the need.

Is escape really as numb and hollow as it seems?

When all your escaping is yourself.

Changing out of the man that is you,

And unleashing the chaos inside of you.

I cannot live this insanity,

It's not the way I'm built.

I cannot live while shaming myself anymore.

I'm too consumed with guilt.

I am destroying my temple.

The temple God helped build.

Every piece of my being is consumed and fueled by guilt.

This is not where I belong,

Or who I want to be.

Seems the only one,

Who sees the truth,

Is the most important one,

Thank God I see.

I will work on me.

Who?

To sacrifice your soul,

Just wasting away.

Floating high

Through the haze of time.

Achieving nothing

Nor wanting to be something, anything.

Never knowing how happiness is made through you.

Your sorrow is yourself,

You hate to be you.

It is so heartbreakingly sad

But God knows it's true.

Something great could become of you.

Why is it that everyone else knows it but you.

Start being true to you.

Find the meaning of the word, who.

If you don't understand yourself,

How can anyone else understand you?

Don't you have something to try for,

Or is it being ignored through the sin.

Day by day your indulging in.

A tale of your child's neglect,

Your destruction, your future regrets.

Something no sane person could sit and watch.

Cheating yourself of prosperity

Or any hope for potential.

A lost cause...

It's too hard to have love for someone

Whom is suffering a self-induced insanity...

Warped...doomed...just wasting away.

Feel

I am my greatest companion.

The best friend

I will ever have.

Just God and me were my company

Through my long and treacherous path..

Every person I see,

Every voice that I hear,

Every touch I embrace... Is just for the moment.

They all go away.

My faithful Lord and Angels are the only ones that stay.

Really the only ones I need,

To keep my head up high.

To embrace life,

To love, and to hope;

It all has to be fueled from inside.

Hope floats but could slip right through your fingers,

If your hopeless enough not to try.

We need to feel that life is worth living,

Because in the blink of eye,

We can die.

Gamble for perfection

Every move you take

Every decision you make is chance,

A gamble.

Life is a gamble.

It's all a matter of luck.

There is always someone with a better hand.

Always someone who thought of a better plan.

The longer we stay still,

The longer failure remains.

Nothing will ever change.

Everything will always remain the same.

The more we try

The more we realize

That life's too short to just waste away

No one promises another day,

But if you live to see it,

You did something right today.

I use my faith for guidance and comfort.

If I feel it inside,

It must be truth

Denying that part of you is easy,

Especially in youth.

If I could start all over I would.

Start with the knowledge I once never used.

It was ignored while staring me in the face.

Now my search for spirituality

Is more like a race.

We all grow I guess in our own time.

Though time doesn't give me time for perfection.

I gamble with decisions on my perfection.

Wish I knew

I close my eyes, and wish I knew

How to be, closer to you

How to let the pieces

Of my painful life go

Like in with the new

Out with the old

How do I forgive myself

For being a person of sin

Is it ever too late to let God in

Is there going back and fixing

And are we ever really fixed

Are we just drifting by

Catching ourselves before we sink

I turn to You Jesus

Help me let you in my life

I long to live through your love

As I long to follow your truth and life

Breathe into me Your love, Your goodness, strength

Let me grow through you

And learn how to really live

Plan

If you fail to plan, you plan to fail.

It's motivation, it's determination.

Just a prayer from my heart,

And hope in my soul.

I need to know I can make it,

Lord knows I will never let go.

I cry because happiness is something I have never known.

Something I think I will never feel.

So I just pray, and try, and wait,

To see if I can heal.

Will I always mourn every day of my life?

Or will the good overpower the bad someday.

Will I be able to touch someone else,

The way that God touched me.

I wish all the people in the world

Could feel my love for people in the world.

Really know my heart, mind, and soul.

Know that I would sacrifice myself to save someone else.

Truly I can't give something if I have nothing.

May I learn to succeed.

And become something.

Someone to be proud of

Someone with a plan...

Another down

Another addict down,

How many more to go...

What's the point in living if you just ignore your soul?

What's the point in being,

If you're not anything at all...

Just a numb zombie in the form of a person.

Just a hollow empty shell..

Every needle you stick in your arm,

You're already dead...

Inevitably you will be.

There was nothing anyone with sense could say,

To make you realize you've drifted away...

Nothing anyone who cared could do,

You have to want better within you.

Every way out offered

You should have taken it...

Sadly, now, you didn't make it...

I've seen it time and time before,

Nothing will get better if you don't close that door!!!

The door to insanity,

The door to destruction...

Ultimately, now, your gone like so many others.

You thought you could beat the odds,

Or you didn't think at all..

Why did heroin kill you all??

Stir of echoes

How do we stop the stir of echoes

That swarm inside our heads...

The frustration, the confusion,

While all awhile trudging ahead.

Knowing the sin we're indulging in,

And yet doing nothing to change it.

I know better than the wrong that I do,

And I will take the steps to change it!

I can only save myself.

No one else seems to listen.

I could fall all over again,

In the end it's my personal mission...

Chaos right now, is so the reality of many.

Although truth is what we make it...

If your faith is truth, and your soul is strong,

Nobody but you can break it..

Life is truly what you make it.

Somebody

Losing myself through the craze of life..

Feeling something is missing...

I think I lost my ambition..

I don't know if I can grow better than I am right now..

I don't know if I am able to be proud of where I am in society..

I long to be better than the broken heart I was raised to be..

I want to be known for something memorable.

Leave my mark, sing my song, make an impression...

Be cared about, be thought about...

Never am I thought about,

But I am here,

And I fear,

No one thinks I am special..

Just me who the world calls,

A nobody...

Peace

Frustation and aggravation is corrupting my mind.

Digging my way out of this hole,

But it's taking too much time.

I guess it's fine,

You do the crime you do the time

True happiness and comfort is always hard to find.

Always on this money chase,

The constant race I know will never end.

Every time I see things look up

It feels like just pretend.

There's always a dead end,

Success is always so far away .

I struggle here, I suffer there,

I battle every day!

A little piece of some peace

Is all we need up in these streets.

A little hope for the lost

Who have always paid the cost.

A little love for the lonely,

Everyone needs a homie.

I wish I could save everyone including myself,

But I alone can't move a mountain,

I need a little help.

We're all selfish people

With a touch of evil,

Trying to do Gods will

But getting lured by the devil.

Life's like digging a hole without a shovel,

We're grateful for the handouts, living ghetto.

While walking down a lonely road,

Living a lonely life.

Always trying and always failing

When we're trying to do right.

We all have gifts that we're not seeing and not using

We're all just drug abusing.

Don't even see possibility

Or dream to define your destiny.

We all should see,

We could change the world,

If we combine our minds.

Instead of fighting each other and committing crimes.

A little piece of some peace

Is all we need up in these streets.

To change our lives

We gotta compromise,

We gotta take our time,

We gotta do it right.

We gotta come together

We're not here forever,

But always remember,

Never say never..

Always open your heart

And open your mind,

Wake up and find yourself,

The test of time.

Unhappiness is an army

There's no harmony, and everyone lies to me.

Trying to be successful but not with a goal

We're all holding on to hope and faith

If it isn't already gone.

Life hurts young

It's been so long,

Since I have felt relief.

Pieces of my sanity are flaking off

And landing all over my feet.

Will we ever know peace?

Saved broken

Through this life of evil

This life of pain

I have seen the light and found my way

Thinking everybody hates me

By the way they raised me

I was just a little kid living a life of hurt

But now I'm stronger than ever

Nothing can stop, all the hope in my heart

I am stronger, I'm so brand new

Now that I embrace your life

Now that I found you

I have sat and cried so many times

Feeling all alone

Ignoring all the little signs

That God's love is my home

When not knowing where to turn

As a child with a broken heart

His love is always here

It found the way into my soul

Now I will never let go

Now I'm stronger, than ever

Nothing can part, me from my Faith in my heart

I am stronger, life is so brand new

With my soul filled with his light

I found my way to a beautiful life

What an amazing thing

When you find your way out of the dark

That through every tear that falls

To our Lord it called

Someone cared about me all along

I just had to pray to call

Now I'm stronger, than ever

Nothing to take me apart

From the love in my heart

I am stronger, and so brand new

I built myself a better life

Through all the torture of my soul

I am healed

I am whole

Stained memories

Memories of childhood are sadness

All of this time I thought that I healed

Sometimes I still feel damaged.

The past still haunts my mind at night

I think of what has been done to my life.

Why in my heart do I still feel like a child

Slapped in the face and stabbed in the heart.

You think you overcome

Keep on going and trudging on.

Inside the heart is still filled with sadness

I wish I could forget my past and all it's madness

Replacing the pain with gladness   .

Though I forgive all who have wronged me

It doesn't fade any of the scars.

How do we succeed in life

When nobody teaches you the world.

One thing is for certain

I will overcome this curse.

Stained memories are only my history

Maybe my tears will stop flowing.

At this point it's not about where I came from

It's about my journey and where I am going.

Wreckage

Broken down

Again and again

Beaten my head against the wall

Wishing I could talk to a friend

I need someone to be here for me

Through all this wreckage

I must climb out of

Just a lending hand

And an open heart

I need someone to care

As a feel so alone

And misdirected, misguided

Someone better is out there

Maybe they wait

For me to pick up the shattered pieces of my soul

Only then will I be whole

Rain Wash away

Let this rain, rain

Wash away my worries

Rinse away my pain

Your sun will shine on me

And give me strength another day

All this Fury

All this rage

It only brings me down a way

As you fight the battles within

Darkness tries

To lure you in..

As I lick my wounds to heal

This anger, this grief

I don't want to feel...

Let this rain, rain

Rinse away my worries

Wash away my pain

Oh rain

Cleanse me to the core

I don't want to sin anymore

Engross me in the lessons of my soul

Rain away, rain away

On our world

Your sun will shine on us

In a supernatural way

Until it fuels your heart

And learn to manifest and focus on today

I don't want to stay

In the darkness of this cloud that follows

I don't want to deny my God

And let this shallow life turn me hollow

Sometimes reality

Is a hard pill to swallow

Let Your rain, rain

Wash away all worries

Rinse away this pain

Oh rain, rain

The sun will shine

On another day

I need Your glorious healing

Through the water dripping and cleansing

Testing me through time and space

To cleanse my being

To change my face

Everywhere

The beauty of everything

Always existing,

The way God had planned

Wanting to teach you

Just put out your hands

Feel the spirit of this world

Resonate in your soul

The joyful song of the birds

Instinctively knowing how to survive

Which way to feed and go

God is in all He created

You can feel it though it's not seen

Just like how we breathe

We cannot see air

Though we know it's there

Sometimes you just know and believe

That feeling inside of love

That's fuzzy and warm

That spreads into every piece of me

The Holy Spirit

We can't deny the truth

God's beauty is everywhere

I long for His Grace

To take all doubts away

Opening the eyes of His people

More and more each day

Faith is everything

Faith is everything

Your daily food

The feeling inside that

Connects into everything

Knowledge and love that ignites

Our hearts into everything

Keep striving for your best self

Only then will you receive

The greatest of God's help

Falter no more

With the strength of our Lord

Do the works of the heart

Love without boundaries

If you are chosen

Play your part

My healer

The beauty of your love

It warms the depths of my soul

My dearest Lord I swear

From Your word

I will never let go

Growing stronger by the day

I put you always in my heart

Somehow I am happy

Though my life had fallen apart

I trust in you and know I must

I can feel what I am destined for

You are merciful and just

Holding open the door

Take away the damage from this life

Help me to know

And to see

What is right

My healer of my mind,

Body, and soul

Without my Faith

I will never be whole

Without your love we simply wouldn't be

I can feel You

Raining your healing

Upon me

Lead the way

Oh my Lord

Just lead the way

Since I found you

My life has changed

No longer feeling estranged

I will never be the same

As you lead me

Out of my own living hell

Step by step you

Taught me to stand tall

Strip away my shame

And to love myself

The way you selflessly love me

I cherish your love

You held my hand

When I was broken

I realize the greatness and beauty of my name

Lit for me the way

Obstacle

Don't let me stray, Lord

From the path that I belong

There's someone trying to mess up our plans

Who dislikes my growth

And criticizes my change

He wants to keep me his victim

Still trying to steal my joy

Trying to dull my shine inside

Though he won't succeed

Still he reigns his lies and delusions

Chipping away at me

Little by little

Until he thinks I'm weak enough to fall

Don't let me fall for it my God

Our existence is greater than

Wasted souls that can't believe

What they don't see

There was no waste my God with me

Grateful am I you helped me see

All of the things I could not be

Never could I turn away

Faith is the world to me

God's healing

Head up, head up

I have to keep my head up

I have to keep my spirit up

Or I will drown in this flood

Of all emotions I cry

When I can't stop wondering why

And I need the pain of the past to die

I know my Lord hears my cries

I need to have His healing

To feel the beauty of grace

It is a beautiful feeling

Unchain me from this world

Oh Lord, and let my spirit soar

Free me from the bondage

That has always tried to break me

Cultivate me, remake me

I am clay in your hands

Open my eyes and heart

To your ultimate plan

Praise

You know my name

You know my heart

Since your hands sculpted this face

And every other part

From the beginning your plan unfolded

For my souls despair in this life

And my triumph over it

The depths of your love is inconceivable

The more I learn of You and your Grace

It's almost unbelievable

Nothing so beautiful has ever been shown

In this twisted wicked world

The Love You give just has to be known

By Your Grace I am made whole

These blind eyes finally can see

I honor you from the depths of my soul

Oh My Lord I am in awe

Amazed and perplexed

By the mercy and love

Complexity and divinity

The more I learn the more I crave

I will forever ever praise you

With every fiber of my being

Purpose

Just like life, turmoil brings out cause

As heartache overtakes your mind

You learn to turn to God

All my poetry, through everything

It's all my pathway to my faith

You have to feel pain and betrayal to know love

Life's path is more evident

When you are looking down the wrong road

You know true love, when you experience the mediocre or tainted

You appreciate when you have been without

It all just falls into perspective

My poetry reflects my life's greatest losses

And also my greatest gains

All the glory goes to my creator

Keep you

Through space and time

Eternal and light fire

Flowing the beauty

Of his grace and love

Showing me myself

Through the splendors of his love

Universal in all He created

Breath-taking, as my heart opens

As wide as it can be

Connected into all that I am and see

Into every person's spirit

Connected in his marvelous love

Working the Holy Spirits

Awe inspiring magnificent power

To have, and to love

Breathing into you, His truth

The Trinity want to keep you

Our God wants to transform you

Be a leader in this day, in this hour

Power

I feel your power

Lord, I feel that power

Every second, every hour, Your power

I know Your power flows through me

Showing me who I should be

Your love shines within me

Lighting everything I see

Fueled by passion in Your loving light

Of all that can be

Your destiny

I'm in that destiny

For all You had for me

For us

Shining Your light across the seas

It's not just for me

This was Your plan for me

Now I'm free, to soar in Your dreams

Mysticism, intoxicating,

I will bring them to Your light

It just might save their life

Your power flows within me

Telling me whom I should be

Your power is exploding

Clearing a path for me

When I'm living in your light

I know I belong on Your side

Let me shine Your light

For all the world to see

In Your power of all I can be

They can see that change in me

Thought

Turn on the light of thought

The wonder and example

Of how good our God really is

And how to love each other

Without boundaries, without judgment

We are supposed to live in harmony

When my fire burns for the world

Exemplify me, fuel me up

Igniting a fire within our hearts

Spreading our knowledge

And the beauty we have learned

We thirst, we thirst

Only your will and word

Will quench this thirst

We need to know how to really love each other

Without boundaries, in respect, and grace

Fuel us up, igniting fires within our hearts

Spreading the awesome knowledge of Your Love

Guide us in every thought

Don't break

I can't let anything break me down

My own daily battle, to enjoy my life

Through so much heartache and so much headaches

I must remain strong

No matter how wrong people are to me

Or how forgiving in my life I've had to be

In the end, I do it for me

I can't shut everyone out just because in my life

They were wrong to me

Just because they didn't really know

Truly didn't see

I am the one who lives in my reality

I can choose to suffer inside

Or turn God for healing and understanding

So much in this world is wrong

But this life is all I have

Building my faith strong

Those who suffer, will truly know happiness

The wisdom of my journey

I take nothing for granted

I have felt like I had nothing in this life and no one

I know that just having life and being me is a blessing

That and faith is all I have

It's all anyone has

Coming

I see Angels coming

There is something in the air

I am aware, things are changing

We can feel it in our hearts

The seventh seal is now a part

And I know, in my soul

Our God is working now

Manifesting change within our souls

We know we can change this world

That is purpose, that is His goal

We pray for the world

Oh for the souls who didn't know

The future of our people is in His hands

We need to let go and let God

And I see it every day

God is moving now, in every way

We know the fight is not done yet

I see Angels coming

They're here to protect

God is changing it all

Remain mighty, never fall

In His might we can never fall

Future is today

I must never shut out my faith

I am drifting in my sea of worry

Drowning in my debt of living

Just existing, the allusions of life

As always I need

My Lord to guide me

My future starts today

Blindly I can't seem to find my way

Or have the strength to fight

Although I am filled with gratefulness and gladness

Somehow this world steals your happiness

And fills you with negativity

We need to break the chain, and let it all out

So there is more room for the good

We all need to just let go, and let God

We need to be strong, and focus on what's important

Happiness, and love, unity in diversity

Our existences, ultimate destiny

In beauty, grace, it will be a magical place

It starts with me, it starts with you

To show and lead a better way

The future is today

Fueling

You are always in my heart

Fueling love within my soul

I have ignored you in my life before

Now from your loving light, I will never let go

Oh Lord, you lit the way when I was lost

Now I found myself and I found my cause

With all the damage I have done to myself

Through grace I am made new

Through you Jesus, I am found

Oh Lord, I could never turn my back on you

I realize I am a part of you

Each human is a cell in the body of God

It is such a transforming thing

When we embrace His love

With an open mind, and open heart

Miracles can happen, if you do your part

Embrace the beauty in His beautiful world

Love our planet, hear the song of the birds

When your eyes are opened to the glories in this life

It's so easy to let yourself be fueled with God's love

Then everything just goes right

Never turn away

Let your kingdom shine in me

Help me soar above all, with Your wings

Your wings made of hope

For our way back to truth

We can always find our strength in You

If our hearts cry out to You

I want to be like Jesus

We need to be like Jesus

Only He, can open your mind to your destiny

We need to break the negativity, and be free

It's all so clear in my heart of hearts

We need to wake up and play our part

Evolving knowledge and graciousness

Around the Earth

It's been our mission since our birth

Break free, break free

I know that Jesus lives in me

Working to transform this wicked existence

His plan will reign, without our permission

There is no way, I can ever turn away

My Lord, O Lord

My heart, my mind

Will never break away from you

When I feel Your hope inside

Break free, break free

I know Jesus lives in me

Only His love will open your eyes to really see

All we are and are destined to be

In thought

I have been disconnected

Wrapped up in my thoughts

Doubting myself everyday

I despise me today

How do I let go of my shame

How do I heal, this self-inflicted pain

Lord, I need your strength

Your loving flow of power

I am just so tired of being tired

I'm so exhausted from worry and doubt

How oh Lord, do I heal my heart

Teach me to let go

Of the sorrow in my soul

I know I need You, life is taking it's toll

Just to love my life, I need Your healing light

Always needing You to control my life

Give me the confidence to be

Who You meant for me to be

You are the leader in this search for me

One day

Your eyes were a window to eternity

I know you will always be with me

My memories of you will last forever

And One day with God

We'll be together ♡

Connect

The human soul

Is an amazing part

Sculpted by wonders we can't explain

In each of us, it's art

Something inside me

See's the man-made hell that's all around me

Knowing it's all a test

A test to find our fate

An eternal taste

There's no time to waste

Our spirits can soar above all

Into our purpose we crawl

Through the Holy guide of God's wisdom

Fueled by the love we all can reach

No mountain is too steep

When lifted up in the winds

Resting in creations wings

Heart of mine

This heart of mine

Spreads unconditional love

Through the tests of time

Beating For truth, beating for you

Beating to spread the love of the world

Fueled by the spirit of God's truth

The light of the world

We hold within our hearts

When connected together

A mighty fire will blaze

When our lights shine together

Through the power of God's grace

Humanity surely, will change its face

There is a reason, we were sent to this place

A transformation of heart, soul, and mind through love

For awareness to overcome

This pulse my heart feels

Knows how much God's love will heal

How our entire existence will change

Let the love and healing of the Lord

Fall like rain

Touch a life

Motivated by spirit

To touch a life

Every day

Motivated by love

To spread knowledge

Of the way

I crave direction, everyday

Oh word of God

You are my way

Speaking to my heart

With every page

Showering my spirit with Your truth

Every moment, I am loving You

The most fascinating subject

To penetrate my heart

My mind is captivated and fueled

By Your words and heart

You are my direction, my drive

My source of all experience, of all love

Oh what this spirit of mine

Has overcome

For you

Our most powerful metaphysical creator

Breathed His breath of love into us

Us His living omnipresence

Experiencing all through His divine energy

Learning the world's wisdom

Through infinite time and space

Love is the glue holding existence together

Though most of humanity

Loves not the creation

Most of humanity feels not

The love of our creator

As karma spins is a violent wrath

A reaction to the darkness

That is overloading this place

We are a crazy train flying off the tracks

The word telling us to move forward

Don't look back

Educate each other for this attack

Spiritual warfare is at its peak

We must take our places

It's time to lead

Cure this devil given disease

Your people are on their knees

Lord please

Let us all know, believe, and see

To break down these walls

That make us bleed

So we can bleed for you

Let it be

I have to let it be, and just accept it

Let it be another lesson

Maybe it will coax another confession

Out of the depths of my soul

Layer by layer, I shed the pain

And let go

Let it be

To use the experience to build

A genuine me

River of change

I am wading into

The river of change

Though, it is a struggle to let go

Of what covers my pains

My physical damage

Is past stains, from the hurt

Manifestations of a child's hearts anguish

When weighed down by the hurt

Inside where love still resides

My spirit needs truth, God's truth, the only truth

Layers of sadness shed off, as I learn the way

Emotions stir and flow out

As I let go of more every day

Soon to be floating

On the flowing river

Within the waters I will not shiver

The spirits of creation will be at my needs

A gift to all from the Holy realm

Protecting all hearts as me

Fueled with faith and belief

My faith will grow into a giant tree

With thick roots embedded in the Earth

Penetrating long and immeasurably deep

Watered freely

From the river

Of change

Cries

Cries for our world

Whirl up from the earth

Motivated emotions

Fill the heavens

Moving the core

Of our Creators essence

He moves through the wind

Working if we allow Him to work

Or acknowledge His presence and manifestations

Although doubt conquers many

He hears the hearts call of every

If only they would let Him save

We are all degenerating mental slaves

There is a better way

Call on Him

He will show you

A brighter day

Enlightened

I made a vow to trust God

With every fear, sadness, and worry

All of the sudden, my depression fades

The word, wisdom, and evidence

Of our Divine Creator I crave

My eyes start opening little by little

Sadly, seeing a disturbing picture

Degenerating minds of mankind

Controlled by witches and demonic worship

Herded like cattle into the nowhere

Every life suffers greatly

Due to our own man made horrific destiny

Our leaders are leading the way to destruction

Death of our spirits, our health, our wealth

Keeping us tangled in the web

Of negative powers growing

So many people are going

Down the path we're taught to go

We need to stand up, speak out, and say no

People should know

Life can be a dream land

If you simply shed the pain

And turn to the greatest power at be

He enlightens

And is transforming me

Quilt of humanity

Humanity beautifully knits together

Like a quilt sewn with love

Each fiber stretches across the rest

Together creating the quilt

All threaded together, it's one quilt

Each thread touches the next piece

Such as, each life touches another within humanity

The strength in the fibers are the love of all

Tough and held together, in loves strength

As the love is lessened,

The strength starts to fade

Becoming worn out, and stretched

Creating weakness, creating destruction

One weak piece weakens adjoining threads

A ripple effect ensues

Such as humanity,

Love is the energy holding it all together

As love fades out of the whole

The fibers tattered, it tears a hole

Just as people living loveless,

Spreading despair due to their own broken hearts

Without the love

We fall apart

Here I am

Here I am, I am

Believing in your greatness

Hoping, praying, loving...

Knowing I can be better

You are the reason

For my hearts singing

Enlighten me more, so I can see

Lead the way, to whom I'm destined to be

No more destruction of myself

Crutching and twisting my reality

Every minute, every day

Help me live my life, Your way

Here I am, I am

Trusting in your power

Knowing of your love

Seeking of Your wisdom

Above me, may it shower

Create a masterpiece in me

Let Your loving light

Exude from every piece of me

Here I am, I am

Trusting You to help me be

Lingers

Deep down inside still lingers

The heart of a sad little girl

Who doesn't know why

She was so hurt by this world

Somewhere in my heart, I am still that child

Through the stained memories

My emotions run wild

I must learn from all the pain that it brings

And cleanse my spirit from all the grief

Maybe I've been holding on to the wrong things

No longer am I, or will I be victimized

Not by my father, lover, or any brother

Self-love is key,

For me to stand up for me

That reality is not real for me anymore

So why don't I feel free

Lord, free me from the hell of my past

The heart of that little girl will cry no more

Growing with the spirit, to be

Everything creation planned for me

The poet in the heart

Of every broken person I see

Let them hear the truth in me

Our children

Guide our children

With the wisdom of God's word

Loving every little innocent face

In that unconditional type of way

In loving guidance, maybe they can lead

The way for a brighter day

If taught to rise above

What this world, surely will throw their way

In love, breaking down the borders

Freeing the oppressed from their chains

We can lead our children today

God's loving light, is making a way

To learn to love and protect each other

From a life of karma, so hurtful and shallow

They need this today, not tomorrow

Our children are the future

Shift

Can you feel it?

A shift of happiness inside?

Tremendous emotions and energy

Cleansing your inner vibe?

Ancient emotions pouring out in tears?

Strength for your truth to be spoken?

Can you see it?

The changes in our world...

People coming together in love

When disaster strikes their homes?

Can you sense it?

The powerul shift in your soul..

Crying out every past pain

Just so you can grow?

We shouldn't fight it, nor deny it...

We're evolving at God speed

Finally that time of light,

In humanity

Tap into the light and charge your being...

To find the guidance to live our destinies

We are shifting into who we really are..

Loving our lives, wounds will be scars...

Creation energy is surging from the earth

For us to move on and grow,

For our rebirth

Metaphor of tears

Cleansing of our heart becomes

When our pain streams out in tears

So many people, have held them in for years

Each tear is a rolling metaphor of cleansing

A reminder of what we really are

Spiritual beings, beaten down by a physical world

Living omnipresence in unison

Floating through the sands of time

Building up our hearts pain

As it overcomes us

Let our tears fall like rain

Our living metaphor of tears

Cleansing our spirits

As water cleanses all the same

Every drop filled

With let go pain

Guidance

I need guidance

Through Your Holy light

For all the I wills and I might's

So I know which way

Is wrong or right

Discernment, understanding

The floodgates of Your

Wisdom and love

I will not fight

With you, oh Creator

Life is better than alright

Let me live the glories

Of Your might

With every place I go

Spreading Your loving light

I need

I need your awareness and knowledge

To flow through me

As I need to see

All aspects of life

Through Your loving frequency

Help me, ignite Your love

That never fades away

Burning steadily, away forever

My mind must be focused on You

My heart needs to be fueled by You

As my body needs Your healing

Let It be

Let Your wisdom

Create the best in me

As I streak Your love

For the world to see

I need to feel You in me...

In this space with me

My heart is saturated with love

When You, are in this space with me

Like my pen is guided from above

To transform, Your place in me

My emotions words are heard

Through the dimensions of space and time

Somewhere in me, I know

I was always Yours, and Your love was always mine

In this space with me

I know I live eternity

I know that love can set all free

Magical creation is within us

Though we focus only

On what we can see

It's through wisdom and care

You have planted those seeds

That awareness floods my soul

For every person, floating in love and free

Is Your goal

I can feel it, and I cherish it

When You are in this space with me

Erased

I have erased the past

It never even happened

Creating my own story

By living love in action

I never was hurt

I never was damaged

It's all in my mind

That story is famished

I am strong, I am mighty

Walking in the light

I am able, I am stable

Within my heart and mind

Looking back, is merely a story to tell

No emotions are attached

As if it wasn't myself

I've erased all that doesn't service my purpose today

And anything about me

This world has to say, and has negatively portrayed

In this mindset I thrive

In this thought I stay

God will always clear my way

Ride the tide

The rushing tide, within our minds

Drifts us away, from truth and faith

We so rarely hear

God's ultimate words

The keys have been buried

Throughout the years

Even faster, humanity drifts away

Everything we are and are supposed to feel

We can sense it fade away

Spirits are waking everyone

So we can build a better today

God's way, the best way

Heal the wounds of yesterday

Then ride the tide

Without the pain

Only then, are we really living

Only then, we are truly free

The infinite love of Jesus

Will set all free

Drenched

Drenched by the tears of letting go

I'm feeling whole

Released now of years

Of heartache and held in tears

It's so evident now, I know

Going back, I could never go

Rising higher within myself

I can feel spirits presence

We are never by ourselves

Drenched by the tears of letting go

So clearly I can see

Creations ultimate goal

My mind clearing in unison

With my bleeding heart

Entity of my being soaring

Higher than ever before

Letting go, and letting God

Changed my entire existence, my purpose

I was filled with the most powerful love

Pushing out every little pain

Every piece that doesn't belong

Healing me up the ladder

A new reality, I have won

Drenched in the tears

Of letting go

Your way

Your light is in us

Your energy

Is in all things

Let us shed our built ideals

So we can absorb You in

Connect to Your wisdom

And all that we are and see

A priceless player in this reality

Follow me

Let us light the way

Showing others how to break their chains

Living life a whole new way

The way Jesus taught, lived, and prayed

Following His words

Illuminates our way

We need His truth and wisdom

To heal our people today

Ultimately changing away from our ways

Your love will lead the way

Tell me why

My friend

Walk with me

Talk with me

Tell me why you cry

Believe my words

When I speak

Of the beauty in the depths of your eyes

Every bad thought, emotion

That you just hold inside

Only leads to your minds demise

Listen when I say

Put it all in the hands of God

This is the time to pray

To truly feel alive

My friend, tell me why

You can't achieve, all you desire

All you have ever dreamed

We just need to know, and believe

My friend, you can always turn to me

To shed the light

When you can't see

Tell me why you lack faith inside

I will show you when you fall

In God you will rise

Floating

Shame and pain

Have evaporated away

Carried away in the winds

Dissipating into the vastness of space

Sorrow, regret, and injustice

From my eyes have dripped away

Through the streams of tears

They float away in the waters

Into the deepest depths of the Earth

Negative energies leave me more

When focused on love inside

A restoration of my heart and soul

Into the abyss, my pieces

My blackness goes

As I wisp through the sun rays

Floating in the clouds

Looking down at beautiful creation

Cherishing the oneness we have found

Beautiful beginning

A glimpse of enlightenment

Compels me to love

Fueling me to reach out

I realize how much I long to help

I may not know you, but I love you

I may not have looked into your eyes

There is still no doubt, their beauty

When I love myself

I can truly love others

Really seeing myself

Shows me how to see others

Knowing the words of Jesus

Teaches me how to live

How to love, how give

Coming together and coexisting

Is the beautiful beginning

Universal truth will flicker your flame

Flooding your memory, stimulating your brain

You can feel it energize within you

Don't let this world lie to you

The world's teachings are false

There is only one truth

If you seek it

It will find you

For a time

The timeless facts were buried

Humanity has been digging

As the leaders try to steal our shovels

Gratefully, with the right intent

We are untouchable

On time

With time gone by, I realize

Generations have been

Spoon fed lies

Illusions are creating

What we see as reality

Therefore, I am instigating

My own allusions

I am drawing

My own conclusions

Preparing myself,

For spiritual war

We are slaves,

Within this world

Within our minds

Free yourself

The love of Jesus

Is always on time

The beauty

Words cannot contain

The beauty of His grace

The power of His love

And how it sets my soul ablaze

I am free

Knowing the love Jesus has for me

How every breath I take

I have the most secure security

We are loved beyond defining

It's amazing how the spirit works in our timing

When we are ready for Him, so is He

Helping us through eternity

The greatness of Jesus

Can mostly be felt

Flooding our hearts

Pushing out self-made impurities

Healing us

Cleansing us of negative energies

With the truth of Jesus

Life can truly start

In each of us

He is a part

What more could He do

To prove

We have His heart

Knowing

I hear Your voice

In the singing of the birds

I hear Your voice

When rain falls

And cleanses the earth

I hear Your voice

In the roaring thunder

And the absolute sheer power

Makes me wonder

Oh, how beautiful You must be

So glorious and bright

Impossible for stained eyes to see

But gratefully, I live Your glory

I feel Your love

I hear Your voice

In all of life's awes

Strengthening my knowledge

Transforming my soul

Knowing that Your light

Has always been

My home

Sleepy head

Wake up sleepy head

Break free from the matrix

And step out of bed

Flood out the b.s. that's polluting your head

No wonder you're so tired

With all that weight on your back

Don't you know you can give it back

We don't have to march with the crowd

Of spiritual zombies who aimlessly march on

They're numb to the beauty

Their ears deaf to God's sounds

Programmed since birth

To live life in the suffering pond

Wake up sleepy head

Don't you know it's too late when you're dead

The beast in you is stronger, when it's fed

Key to life, feed the right beast

Pick the wrong one and

You become the feast

Sorry

Sorry, there is no longer

A hand over my mouth

When I hear wisdom ring

My heart just wants to shout

Many don't like it

Sorry, that's too bad

Fueled by love and truth

Is the best feeling to have

I'm unstoppable, I'm untouchable

Nothing can ever break me again

Point and laugh all you want

You'll see I was right in the end

I speak with conviction

But only in what I know

Sorry, if I can't let it go

I am living my faith

It's always in my mind

No matter what day

No matter the time

The flame in my heart of faith

Burns brighter and stronger

With each passing day

If your demons don't like it

Step out of my way

Rebirth

When we feel like it's all too much

We need to lay it, at His feet

When our strength to live is gone

No doubt, we need kneel down at His feet

It's the design for you and me

The only way to ever break free

Free of the karmic cycle that has consumed humanity

His love is magical, pushing out the pain

Flooded with His love for us

Undeniably, we forever change

When you are so strongly shown your worth

It's a total renewal of spirit, a complete rebirth

Mind, heart, body all cleanse and grow

Closer, ever still

To the greatest love people will ever know

Laying every piece, at His feet

Is the beginning of being in the   know

Learning the way to live is

Spreading love wherever we go

Together

Do not fear, my child

Did you not hear

I am always within you

Not just close , or   near

I reside in a place inside

Where many have not seen

Look deep inside yourselves

For that spark of life that shines

A tiny piece of ultimate love and heart

That this world tries to bury in our minds

Our collective is damaged

As we sew together a new beginning

Let our hearts create it

Hand in hand, coexisting, and just being

Healing the matrix of time

Patching the fabric of our man-made demise

We are the future

One step at a time

Let us grow closer to truth

And all step together this time

Not with ego, not with pride

Make a move, or fall behind

Knowing it's all for and through

The glory of

The living mind

Lies, all lies

Into the fire,

We burn

As this planet,

Slowly turns

All we are,

And all we've learned

Is lies, all lies

We were made to soar these skies

Let love lift us high

So our colors can streak the sky

In the ashes of our broken dreams

What we see,

Is what we are

Our limitations dictate how far,

If at all

Reaching out for the impossible

Realizing only then,

Now it's possible

To be my dream,

That daydream

The daydream in my child heart

I saw then,

What my mind would soon doubt

You know what is missing,

After going without

Only waking up to find out

All we think,

And all we're told life is about

That it's lies, all lies

Told to us,

So we don't try

To ever reach our heights,

And soar the sky

From universal truth,

We have been denied

To even know ourselves,

When we're told who we are

The more we love,

The more we lift each other high

Let us streak our colors far and wide

From the abyss to the sunrise

In the eyes of the most high

We're shooting stars,

Lighting up the sky

Dancing to the rythme of glorious life

To lift us higher than before

To the core

Let us soar,

For You

Calls

My heart calls out

As I close my eyes

I beg You Lord

Knowing You hear my cries

May Your love control my heart

May Your wisdom open my mind

Show me Your reason

Guide this life of mine

Pieces of me

I'm falling apart,

Piece by piece

Unraveling slowly,

Down to my feet

What once held me together

Is now weak and brittle and torn

But for every part of me that dies

A better piece is born

As pieces of me break,

I heal

Blindly stepping forward

Lured by how I feel

Feeling from my center,

My core

Seeing life like never before

I'm falling apart piece by piece

Like a waterfall rushing on

There is no stopping me

Like perspiration,

I drip away

The purpose for me,

I have strayed

At the bottom,

In my Faith I am saved

Like a puzzle I will be repieced

Into a stronger, smarter

Better me

To see

Poisoned by every breathe we take

Had my mind comatosed,

I am now awake

I am not too far gone to see

I won't march with the spiritual zombies

I will not live like everybody

After feeling and seeing the light

I felt it blanket a warmth on my skin

Then sink it's way in

To penetrate my soul

All that darkness had to go

The endless battle of life

Of wrong or right

Of darkness or light

Where is your heart,

And is it right

Is it stuck on the ego

Do you harbor evil

Or are you a spreader of love

Do you hold emotions inside

Truly we are our own success or demise

Only receiving what we put out

What is it we have

Swimming around inside

Besides pride

Is your mind believing all the lies

Or are you focused on love

With your eyes on the prize

I am not too blind to see

Without the spirit of truth

How my life would be

And how we are loved through eternity

Always will it fuel and define me

To help others lift the veil to see

Everything we are

And were meant to be

Father of my soul

Father of my soul

Unveil the love

That You have for us

And from it

May I never let go

Only You

I sing because I know

From Your children

You will never let go

I dance because I feel

The joys in my life

Only You make real

Align

Lord, you are my heartbeat

You are the ground beneath my feet

Align me in your ways

So I can live for you today

May I walk closer to your purpose

More and more each day

Fueled in your love

Please shape me

I am your clay

My place

I take my place

Always seeking your face

While every moment

Blessed in your grace

This journey has rescued me

From my own self-induced death

As my soul was reborn

Now, we strengthen my mind and flesh

Seeking truth between the lies

In answering my calls

I was given new eyes

As I follow the spirit and guide

Never again, feeling empty or broken inside

Through faith and unity we thrive

Healing through your love

Hugged tightly in the splendors of your light

Feeling with conviction

Your power and your might

Needing always, your guidance

To walk this path right

Help me be a great soldier

In this physical, spiritual fight

Fortunate

Thank you God

The puzzle pieces of life keep coming

As the big picture,

All perceptions

Keep changing and growing

As I always live through your love

Keep learning and going

Knowing that now is the time

Of Your Divine healing and molding

How fortunate can we be

To feel our way in Faith and see

Beyond the fog of this illusion

To end the matrix of the world's delusions

I learned to be a vital part of my own solution

Trying to learn from Jesus's words and perfection

Living in the peace of Your Holy protection

Oh how blessed could I be

I prayed for sight

Now clearly I see

A mighty oak has grown

From faith's planted seed

The light is and always will be

Alive in me

Told

This world told me who I was

I believed those lies for so long

Building myself on the faulty foundation

A foundation of self judgement and shame

Knowing something damaged in me

Needed to change

I am who I say I am

Who God showed me I am

That undeniable truth

Changed my opinion of me

That undeniable truth

Penetrates into all that I feel and see

I realize now how I am the source

Of all of my miseries

Time to tear down

What this world has helped me build

Renewing my mind

With the wisdom of the word

The keys to our own success

We each truly hold

Working daily on myself

Is how I change my world

Clarity

The labyrinth of the mind

Entangles us, through space and time

Through clouded eyes we perceive

Ego's too inflated to receive

The gift of truth is for me and you

To embrace, embody, become

In all we think and do

Turning our hearts and minds to the maker

While this world embodies the taker

Taker of purity, stealer of joy

Separating us from the Light

So life is impossible to enjoy

We crawl through the maze

With distorted senses, in sight

Clarity comes when God turns on your light

Lighting our way

Each step in each day

Once given a taste

How can we turn away

Glorious

Oh, this glorious day

Nothing can take

This joy in my heart away

The place I stand right now

Used to look so far away

Oh, this glorious life

I pursued the word

And the truth came alive

Bringing me ever closer

Directing and guiding my stride

Transforming every dark piece of me

And every dark corner in my mind

In this glorious Light I thrive

This is truly living

This, is being alive

Stillness

Like a dog pulling the leash

My thoughts take lead

Focusing on my egocentric mind

Distracting me to waste my energy and time

I have to strengthen my mind

Train myself to look inside

To tap into the spirit

That lives in me

Let the ripples of thought

In my mind grow clear

Only then

Can I truly hear

Stillness of my mind

Direction of my spirit

Train me Lord

To be it and feel it

Lead me to your still waters

In the moment

While I quench my thirst

Truth drips from every word

Cleansing every impure piece in me

Guide me closer

Every day

Strengthen me for your purpose

So I am ready for this fight

Standing tall in this battle of the mind

In your wisdom

I truly shine

Printed in the United States
By Bookmasters